A TALE FOR PARENTS:

In 2012 our Siamese cat, Coco, died and for the first time in 20 years the Thomas household was "catless". Though I enjoyed the "litter box-free" lifestyle for a time, soon conversation turned to the search for a new furry family member. So it was that, while looking for a replacement Siamese, we turned up at a local animal shelter hoping that someone might have gotten tired of the ear-piercing yowls and put their Siamese up for adoption.

During that search however, we noticed in the corner of one of the shelter's rooms, a young silver tabby-type cat that didn't look like he'd be on anyone's short list of kitty contenders. Touring the shelter, we kept coming back to this wide-eyed kitten that desperately wanted a home. After hearing his unique backstory and falling victim to his waif-like expression, we decided to take a chance with "Junior" (the name given to him upon his arrival at the shelter).

This is his story. His tale is one of abandonment, redemption, and tough love; experiences that we all deal with in our lives, even when we're too young to recognize and fully understand them.

Junior (whom I later renamed Tiggy) shares our home with his "brother-cat" Chewy (the replacement Siamese) and continues to make life a little more interesting each day. I hope that you and your child enjoy his story; *The Tale of Tiggy the Tabby.*

Roy Thomas
Rosedale, Maryland
Spring - 2015

<u>THANKS</u>

To my friends Shannon Baker and
Sharon Mager for their editorial input
and encouragement.

To Drew and Kimberlea Baker and
their children Sabrina, Jake and Dory, for being
my "test audience" for this material.

And most of all,
to my wife Elaine
my primary cheerleader,
confidant, proofreader
and encourager in this effort

The Tale of Tiggy The Tabby

PART I

How a Homeless Cat

Found a Family

This is the tale

of Tiggy the Tabby

who, when we first met him,

seemed a little bit crabby.

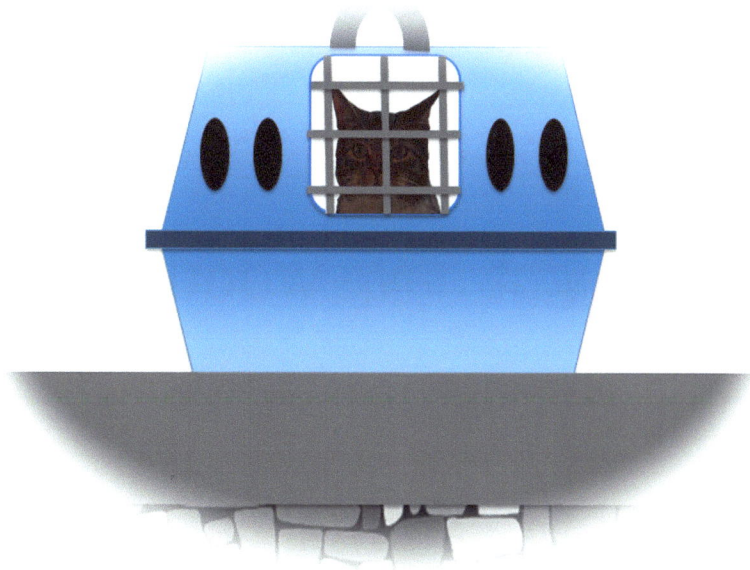

Tig ended up at the animal shelter,

after someone had dropped

him off helter-skelter

in an animal carrier

on a high stone wall

near an old cemetery

in Baltimore.

As Tiggy looked down

from the top of that wall

he might have wondered

"What if I fall!?"

But the animal carrier

he'd been left there in,

kept him safe until

someone rescued him!

Tig watched for a long time

As people walked past.

But none seemed to notice him

until then, at last, a man came by

who spied him up there

and took Tig to a shelter

where he'd get some care.

But what is a "Shelter"?

What's it like there?

Not knowing this

Tig was a little bit scared.

~

But when he arrived

people treated him well.

They gave him a bed,

food and water as well!

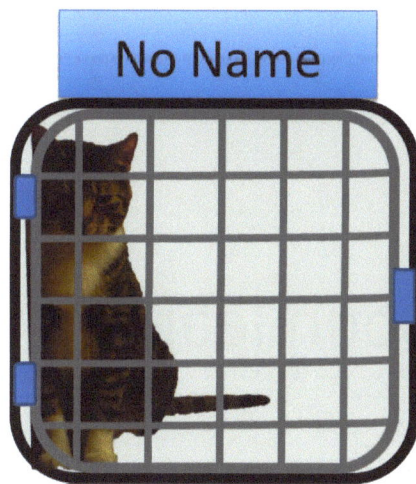

No Name

Not knowing what to call him,

they gave Tig a new name.

"Junior" they named him,

so *"Junior"* he became!

"JUNIOR"

Junior soon learned though

he'd have to stay there,

until someone came along,

who would see him,

and want him,

and give him a home.

But that wouldn't be easy,

for there were MANY cats there

who were also looking

for a family who'd care.

After being at the shelter a day or two,

Junior saw people walking through.

Each was searching

for <u>that</u> special pet

but NO ONE had stopped by

to look at HIM yet!

As Junior waited patiently

he tried to be good,

but his tail kept on waggin'

like he was in a bad mood.

~

When people did stop by

to give Junior a look

they saw his tail waggin',

and that's all that it took!

They kept right on going

because when a cat's tail is waggin'

It may mean he's angry and

might attack like a dragon!

Then a family came by

and liked him right away.

As it turned out,

this was Junior's lucky day.

You see, the mom

of that family wanted a kitty

who would be friendly

as well as pretty.

So when Junior sensed this, he let out a...

And that mother's heart melted and

she said, "We'll take him home now."

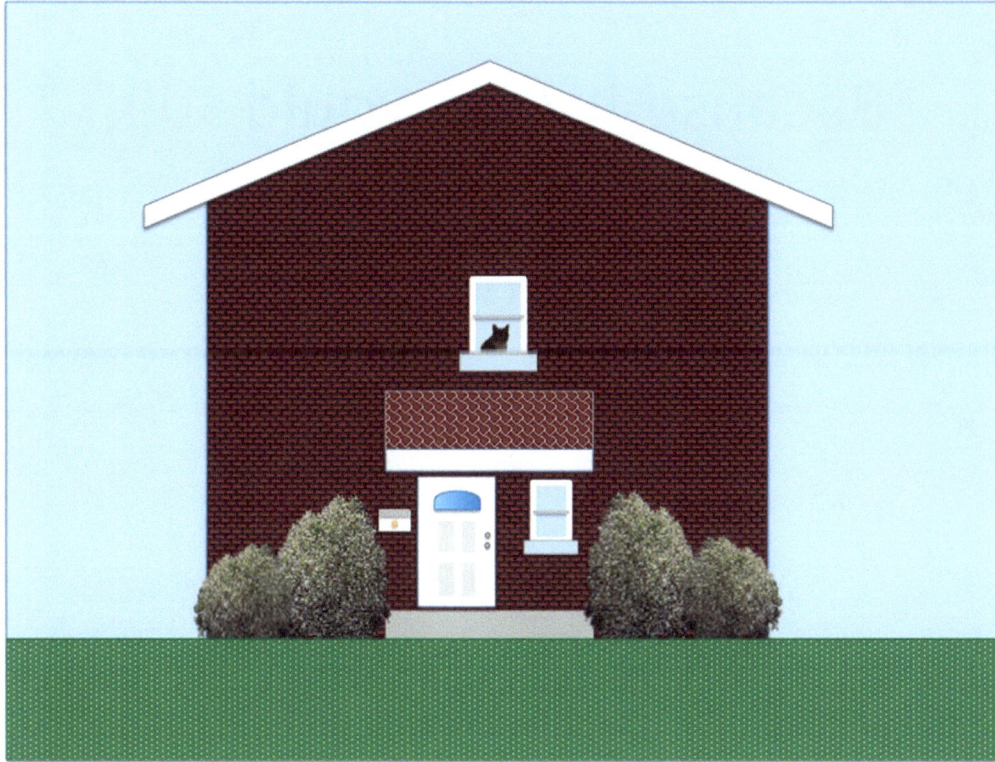

So Junior went home

with the Thomases that day

but that's **NOT** the end of our tale.

Because Junior would still

have to learn

to somehow

stop

always

wagging his

TAIL!

The Tale of Tiggy the Tabby

Part II

Tiggy Tames His Twitching Tail

When Junior went home

with his new family that day,

he still had some problems

along the way.

Perhaps he was frightened,

or he might have been mad.

Or perhaps he was feeling

just a little bit sad.

The Thomases weren't sure

just what was happenin'.

All they knew was that Junior's tail

just kept on waggin'!

When chasing a balloon
you could hear Junior purr,
but his tail kept on waggin'!

While sitting down
happily cleaning his fur,
his tail kept on waggin'!

Hunting for bugs on the front door mat,

his tail kept on waggin'!

Watching for birds
By the window as he sat,

his tail kept on waggin'!

Laying on the sofa while taking a rest,
his tail kept on waggin'!

Doing what he liked worst
or what he liked best,

his tail kept on waggin'!!!

When Mr. Thomas saw

Junior's tail waggin',

he thought his kitty

might be ready to bite.

So he began to call him

by a different name;

"TIGGY",

Because, like a tiger,

Tig had stripes and could fight.

But after awhile

Tig began to calm down

so that now, he enjoys

a good petting!

He even likes to be

rubbed under his chin

because for Tig that's

no longer upsetting!

And so it was Tiggy

learned to love and be loved

and that IS the end of our tale.

But every so often,

though his mood has softened.

Tig can still be seen

waggin' that tail!

The End

Tiggy says....

For more tales, pictures
and all things Tiggy,
visit Tig's Blog at.....

tiggydtabby.blogger.com